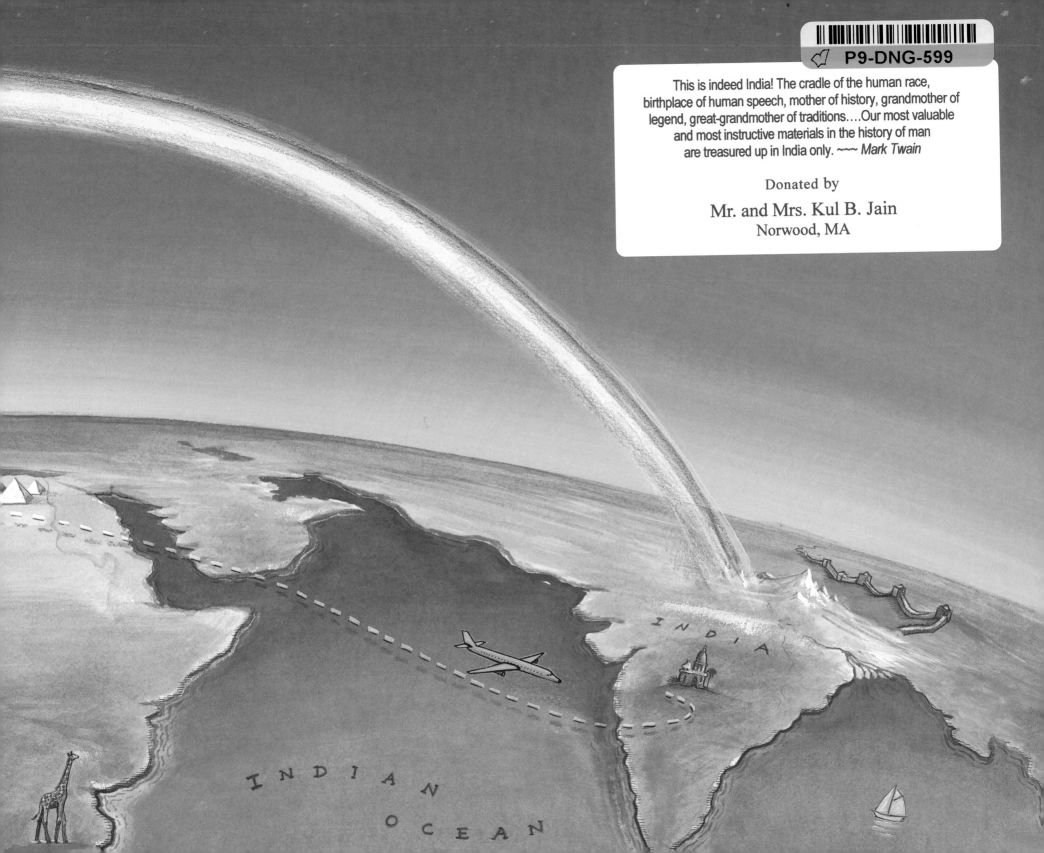

INDIA

INDIAN

OCEAN

This book is dedicated to the silent voice within each of us that prompts us to do what is right.

Finders Keepers?

A True Story in India

Robert Arnett
Illustrated by Smita Turakhia

Atman Press

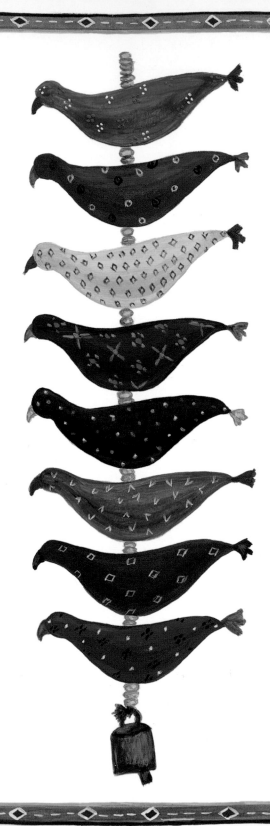

Revised Text © 2013 by Robert Arnett
Illustrations © 2013 by Smita Turakhia

Editors: Smita Turakhia, Doug Glener
Maps: Scott McIntyre

Published in the United States of America by Atman Press
2104 Cherokee Avenue, Columbus, Georgia 31906-1424
AtmanPress@gmail.com
www.AtmanPress.com

Revised Second Edition — 2013
Finders Keepers? is also published in Spanish under the title *¿Es mío?*
Printed and bound in Malaysia by Tien Wah Press

Publisher's Cataloging-in-Publication Data

Arnett, Robert, 1942 -

Finders Keepers? by Robert Arnett
Illustrated by Smita Turakhia

32 p. 28 cm. x 22.5 cm.

Summary: Text and illustrations introduce the traditions, daily life, and values of people of India. Emphasizes important universal values for children. Includes glossary, pronunciations of Indian words, and craft activity.

ISBN: 978-0965290081

Library of Congress Control Number: 2012903513

1. India — Description and travel
2. India — Social life and customs
3. Art — India
4. Religion and Culture — India

J 915.4

A Special Gift For:

_____

From:

_____

A Warm Welcome

In India, a *toran* (TOH-run) is hung over a doorway to welcome God and guests. *Torans* made of fresh flowers and leaves can be seen all across the country.

In the state of Rajasthan (RAH-juh-stahn) in northwest India where this story takes place, *torans* are made of fabric and then decorated with brightly colored embroidery, appliqués, and mirrors. The pennants that hang down from torans represent leaves from sacred trees.

This *toran* welcomes you to *Finders Keepers?*. As you turn these pages, may you enjoy traveling with me to India, a country that has fascinated visitors for thousands of years.

It is hard to look out a window and see the sights of the Indian countryside when every time your bus goes over a bump, you bounce so high off your seat you almost hit your head on the roof!

But there I was, bouncing along on my way to Mt. Abu (Mount AH-boo), a small town on a mountain in the state of Rajasthan.

Some adventurous men and boys who could not get seats inside the bus rode on top with the luggage.

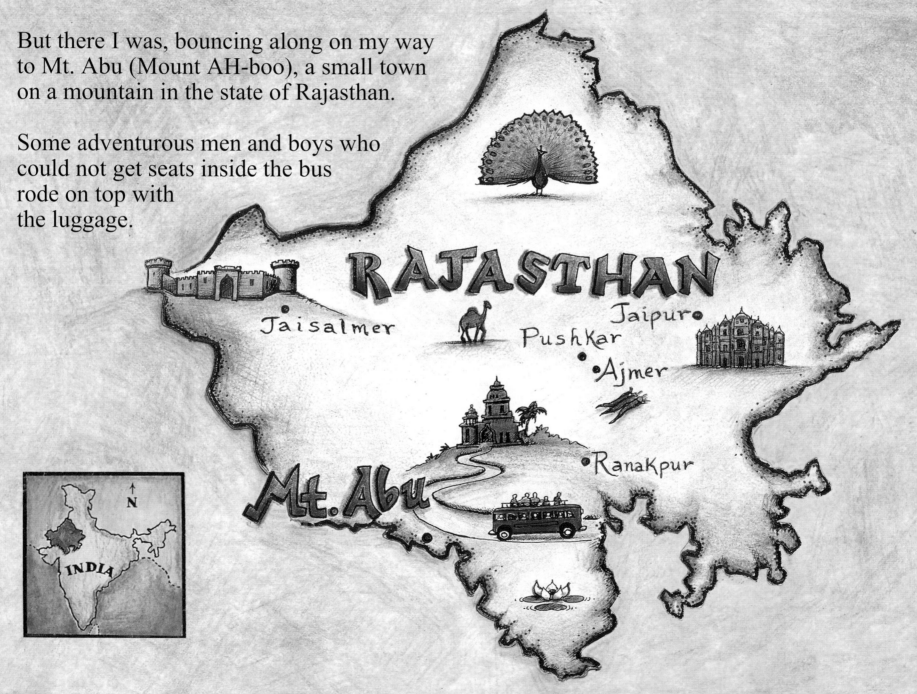

As our bus continued along the winding mountain road, I could see an old fort on top of a steep hill. Its tall, massive walls must have made it difficult to conquer.

Throughout history, the people of Rajasthan have been admired for their bravery, sense of honor, loyalty, and love of freedom.

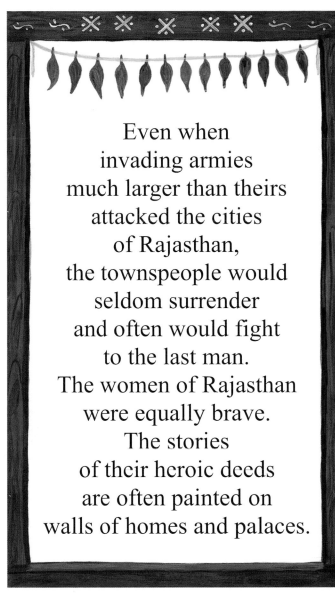

Even when
invading armies
much larger than theirs
attacked the cities
of Rajasthan,
the townspeople would
seldom surrender
and often would fight
to the last man.
The women of Rajasthan
were equally brave.
The stories
of their heroic deeds
are often painted on
walls of homes and palaces.

The bus was packed with people and their belongings. Most of the women were dressed in brightly colored *saris* (SAH-rees). Many of the men were wearing traditional clothes and had colorful turbans on their heads. They had full mustaches that curled at each end. The rainbow colors of their clothing gave the inside of the bus a festive look.

I was surprised to see that when a man took off his turban, on top of his head in a bag was his lunch. It was several flat pieces of bread called *chapatis* (chuh-PAH-tees) and a few carrots. I had never seen anyone use a turban and his head as a lunchbox!

Though most passengers were strangers to each other, some people shared food. Others passed young children and babies around, perhaps to give the mothers a rest. The children were happy and contented to be entertained by total strangers — even by me!

We quickly became like a big family traveling together.

How beautiful to look upon every
and being as dear to you as

one you meet as part of your family
a brother, a sister, or a parent.

We stopped at a roadside rest stop. As we got off the bus, I saw several people pointing up at a tree. Many large bats were hanging upside down from the tree limbs, roosting during the day. The harmless fruit bats, called flying foxes, looked like special effects from a vampire movie.

At a nearby food stall, a man was boiling milk mixed with sugar in a large cauldron over an open fire. I bought a glass of hot milk that he topped with some cream skimmed from the surface of the steaming liquid. To cool it for me, a boy skillfully poured it from one glass to another. The delicious drink tasted like a milkshake. The snacks that were piled high looked appealing, and I bought some to munch on for the rest of the trip.

The next morning in Mt. Abu, I took a bus tour. We went to some of the most famous temples of the Jain (Jane) religion that are known for their intricate marble carvings.

On the way, I saw some Jain nuns and monks walking down the mountain road. In one hand, they were carrying their food containers in a white cotton cloth. With their other hand, they were sweeping the ground ahead of them so that they would not hurt any insects, or even seeds, by accidentally stepping on them.

Their mouths were covered with a small cloth to avoid swallowing even the tiniest insects floating in the air.

Because Jains believe that everything has a soul, they are very gentle people and respect and protect all forms of life.

We also visited a Hindu (HIN-doo) temple that had a statue of Shiva (SHEE-vah) in a symbolic dancing pose. Though Hinduism believes in only one God, it gives names and forms to God's many functions and qualities to help us better understand His mysterious power and intelligence.

To Hindus, Shiva represents God's power that brings all things into creation and takes everything back to its origin when its stay in the world is completed.

The last stop on the tour was a temple built on the highest peak in Rajasthan. It offered a terrific view of the surrounding countryside. While going up the path that led to the temple, I stopped to buy some postcards.

As I walked away, I felt someone tapping my elbow. A young boy with dark hair was standing behind me.

To my surprise, in his outstretched hand was my wallet. I must have dropped it when I bought the postcards.

I offered the boy a reward for returning my wallet, but he would not accept it. I even tried to put some money into his hands, but he put them behind his back. Again, I made an attempt to reward him for his honesty, but he refused. I could not understand why the boy would not take the money.

A man passing by stopped to watch us. I asked him if he could speak English and if he could help me. "This boy found my wallet and returned it to me. Please explain to him that I want to reward him for his honesty."

The man began talking to the boy in their language. After a few minutes, the boy did most of the talking. I was beginning to wonder if either of them understood me.

Then the man turned to me and said, "This boy does not understand why you should give him any money for returning to you what is yours. The idea of accepting a reward for doing the right thing makes no sense to him."

Finders keepers? No way!

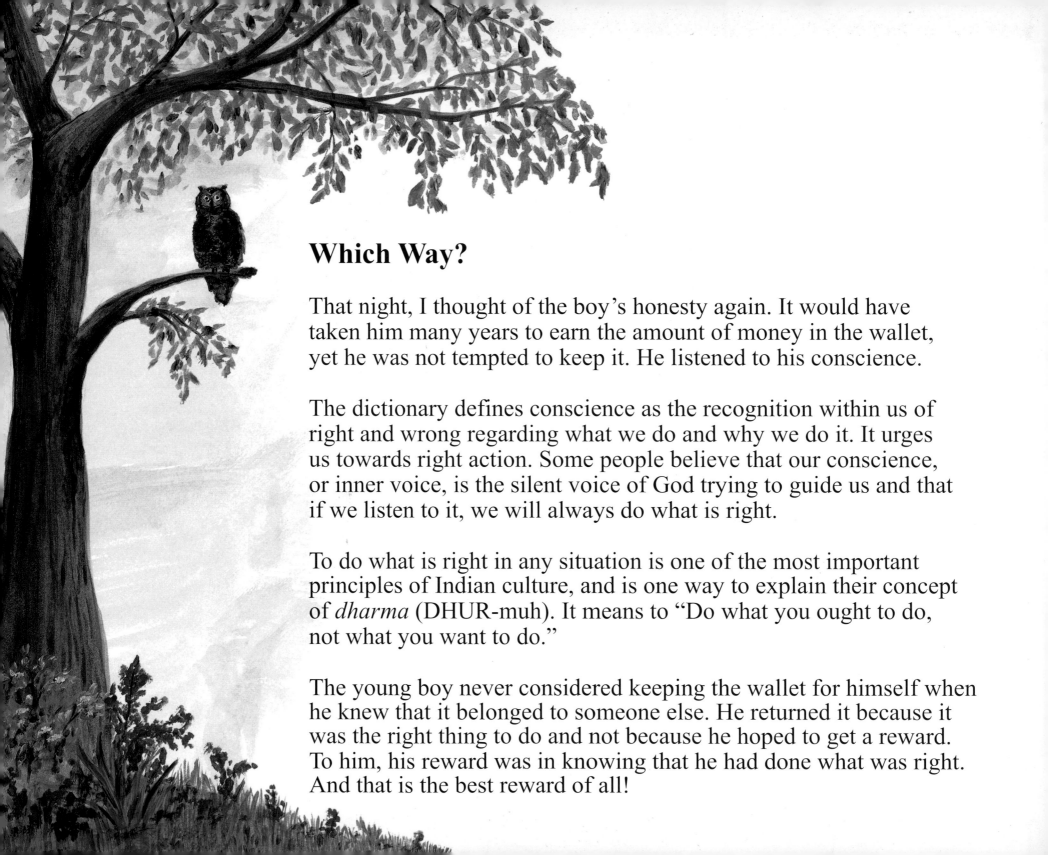

Which Way?

That night, I thought of the boy's honesty again. It would have taken him many years to earn the amount of money in the wallet, yet he was not tempted to keep it. He listened to his conscience.

The dictionary defines conscience as the recognition within us of right and wrong regarding what we do and why we do it. It urges us towards right action. Some people believe that our conscience, or inner voice, is the silent voice of God trying to guide us and that if we listen to it, we will always do what is right.

To do what is right in any situation is one of the most important principles of Indian culture, and is one way to explain their concept of *dharma* (DHUR-muh). It means to "Do what you ought to do, not what you want to do."

The young boy never considered keeping the wallet for himself when he knew that it belonged to someone else. He returned it because it was the right thing to do and not because he hoped to get a reward. To him, his reward was in knowing that he had done what was right. And that is the best reward of all!

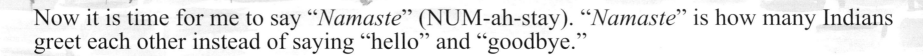

Now it is time for me to say "*Namaste*" (NUM-ah-stay). "*Namaste*" is how many Indians greet each other instead of saying "hello" and "goodbye."

While uttering "*namaste*," they place the fingers and palms of both hands together in front of their chest and slightly bow their head. It is also called a *pranam* (pruh-NAHM) and is a gesture of humility and respect.

In the ancient Sanskrit (SAN-skrit) language, to *pranam*, or to say *namaste*, means "the God in me bows to the God in you" or "my soul bows to your soul."

It expresses the belief that God is present deep within each person, that skin color, race, or religion does not alter the soul-image of God within each of us. So, if we choose to believe this, how could we be unkind to anyone?

So dear ones, I hope you enjoyed traveling with me to India. I enjoyed traveling with you.

"*Namaste!*"

Life is a journey.

Let your inner voice
be your guide.

Treat all who cross
your path with love
and kindness.

Gallantly, reach for
the stars.

Jog Your Memory

chapatis (chuh-PAH-tees)
Thin, flat pieces of Indian bread made of whole wheat flour. It is the most common bread eaten with everyday meals.

dharma (DHUR-muh)
In Hinduism it means to do what is right, regardless of the circumstances.

Hinduism
The largest religion of India. It is one of the oldest religions in the world.

Jains (Janes)
Followers of Jainism. Their religion began in India over 2,500 years ago.

conscience
The inner voice of truth within each of us; the recognition within us of what is right and wrong moral behavior.

Hindu (HIN-doo)
A follower of Hinduism. Hindus believe in only one God, but give Him many forms to make it easier to understand His many functions and qualities.

humility
Not seeing oneself as being more important or being better than others.

namaste (NUM-ah-stay)
Hindu greeting for "hello" and "goodbye." It means "my soul bows to your soul."

pranam (pruh-NAHM)
A custom of placing both hands together in front of one's chest and bowing the head when greeting someone with *namaste*.

sari (SAH-ree)
An 18-foot-long cloth worn by women that wraps around the waist to form a skirt and then drapes over the shoulder. It is worn with a tight fitting blouse.

toran (TOH-run)
A hanging used over a doorway in India as a sign of welcome. It is believed to bring good luck.

Sanskrit (SAN-skrit)
The religious and literary language of ancient India. Sanskrit is the oldest surviving language in the world and influenced many languages of modern Europe.

Shiva (SHEE-vah)
Hindu diety who represents God's power that brings all things into creation and takes everything back to its origin when its stay in creation is completed.

turban
A cloth wrapped around the head to form a headdress for men.

Food For Thought

◫ Would you do something just to please someone else when your inner voice says it is wrong?

When we do the right thing, we feel so good about ourselves that we do not need to seek the approval of our friends.

◈ Do you think you should be paid to help around the house for doing things like keeping your room clean or washing the dishes?
◈ Is it not your responsibility as a part of the family to help with the chores at home?

People around the world do things in many different ways.

◫ What is your favorite ice cream flavor? Do you know someone whose favorite flavor is different from yours?
◫ Which of the two flavors tastes better? Is it possible that their favorite flavor tastes as good to them as your favorite flavor tastes to you?

Not all people think in the same way. Try to understand their way of thinking, even if it is different from yours.

In order to get along better with others, practice looking at things from their viewpoint, and keep an open mind.
They may be right, too, and you might learn something new!

Did You Know?

India is one of the oldest civilizations in the world.

India is the largest democracy in the world.

India has the second largest number of people in the world.

India is one of the most culturally diverse countries in the world. Its religions, customs, celebrations, foods, and even languages vary widely from region to region.

Languages:

India's constitution recognizes 22 official languages.

India has over 1,650 languages that are considered mother tongues, the language spoken in a person's home.

Most students learn to speak three languages in school: English, Hindi (which is the national language), and the language spoken in their own state.

Let's Make a Paper Toran

Materials:

- 6" x 18" strip of green construction paper, or any bright color
- 12" x 18" yellow construction paper, or any bright color
- scraps of brightly colored fabric, or colored paper
- 8-12 small round mirrors, or clear rhinestones from craft store
- 25" piece of string or yarn
- white craft glue
- red masking tape, or any bright color
- scissors
- patterns from this page

Follow the Steps:

1. Using the pattern cut 4 pennants from yellow construction paper.

2. Cut scraps of brightly colored fabric or paper into small squares and triangles.

3. Glue the cut squares, triangles, and rhinestones to the 4 yellow pennants to form designs.

4. Repeat step 3 on the long 6" x 18" strip of green construction paper.

5. Turn the 4 yellow pennants and the 6" x 18" strip of green construction paper so the design is face down. Glue the 4 yellow pennants to the bottom edge of the green strip. Glue the string horizontally across the top edge of the green strip. Let dry.

6. Turn the glued parts from step 5 face up. Tape colored masking tape horizontally across the green strip where the pennants are attached.

7. Loop both ends of the string.

8. Hang the toran over a doorway to give your guests a warm welcome.

The Author

Robert Arnett, a native of Columbus, Georgia, has had an avid interest in India for over 45 years. From 1988 to the present, he has made six trips to India, spending almost two years there traveling around the country and living with Indian families while studying art, culture, and religion.

He is the author and photographer of the internationally acclaimed book *India Unveiled*, a travelogue illustrated with award-winning photography, which has won the Independent Publisher Book Award for Best Travel Book of the Year and the Benjamin Franklin Award for the Best Travel Essay of the year.

Robert Arnett has lectured widely throughout North America, including the Smithsonian Institution, The Kennedy Center, Harvard, Yale, and Stanford Universities. He was a speaker at the Parliament of the World's Religions held in Cape Town, South Africa. He has also given numerous presentations at schools, libraries, community organizations, temples, and churches. He has been interviewed on National Public Radio, Voice of America, and various television programs.

To arrange a presentation in your city, please email Robert Arnett at AtmanPress@gmail.com or contact him directly at 706-323-6377. For more information please visit www.AtmanPress.com.

The Illustrator

The paintings in *Finders Keepers?* come from the hand and heart of Smita Turakhia, a children's illustrator who paints mainly from inspiration and the desire to share the best of India's culture with children. She enjoys bringing India's cultural heritage to life through art and presentations on the culture of India. She was a featured illustrator at The Kennedy Center and has given presentations and craft workshops at the Smithsonian Institution, book festivals, and many schools and libraries.

Smita Turakhia's portfolio includes illustrations for *The Journey to the Truth*, an award-winning DVD that depicted the messages and metaphors of the Bhagavad Gita in the Warli folk art style of India.

Smita Turakhia was born and grew up in Mumbai, India, where she graduated from Nirmala Niketan. After she moved to the United States, she studied fine arts for two years at the University of New Mexico, Albuquerque. She now resides in Texas with her husband. You may contact her at SmitaTurakhia@gmail.com.

Follow the Steps:

1. Using the pattern cut 4 pennants from yellow construction paper.

2. Cut scraps of brightly colored fabric or paper into small squares and triangles.

3. Glue the cut squares, triangles, and rhinestones to the 4 yellow pennants to form designs.

4. Repeat step 3 on the long 6" x 18" strip of green construction paper.

5. Turn the 4 yellow pennants and the 6" x 18" strip of green construction paper so the design is face down. Glue the 4 yellow pennants to the bottom edge of the green strip. Glue the string horizontally across the top edge of the green strip. Let dry.

6. Turn the glued parts from step 5 face up. Tape colored masking tape horizontally across the green strip where the pennants are attached.

7. Loop both ends of the string.

8. Hang the toran over a doorway to give your guests a warm welcome.

The Author

Robert Arnett, a native of Columbus, Georgia, has had an avid interest in India for over 45 years. From 1988 to the present, he has made six trips to India, spending almost two years there traveling around the country and living with Indian families while studying art, culture, and religion.

He is the author and photographer of the internationally acclaimed book *India Unveiled*, a travelogue illustrated with award-winning photography, which has won the Independent Publisher Book Award for Best Travel Book of the Year and the Benjamin Franklin Award for the Best Travel Essay of the year.

Robert Arnett has lectured widely throughout North America, including the Smithsonian Institution, The Kennedy Center, Harvard, Yale, and Stanford Universities. He was a speaker at the Parliament of the World's Religions held in Cape Town, South Africa. He has also given numerous presentations at schools, libraries, community organizations, temples, and churches. He has been interviewed on National Public Radio, Voice of America, and various television programs.

To arrange a presentation in your city, please email Robert Arnett at AtmanPress@gmail.com or contact him directly at 706-323-6377. For more information please visit www.AtmanPress.com.

The Illustrator

The paintings in *Finders Keepers?* come from the hand and heart of Smita Turakhia, a children's illustrator who paints mainly from inspiration and the desire to share the best of India's culture with children. She enjoys bringing India's cultural heritage to life through art and presentations on the culture of India. She was a featured illustrator at The Kennedy Center and has given presentations and craft workshops at the Smithsonian Institution, book festivals, and many schools and libraries.

Smita Turakhia's portfolio includes illustrations for *The Journey to the Truth*, an award-winning DVD that depicted the messages and metaphors of the Bhagavad Gita in the Warli folk art style of India.

Smita Turakhia was born and grew up in Mumbai, India, where she graduated from Nirmala Niketan. After she moved to the United States, she studied fine arts for two years at the University of New Mexico, Albuquerque. She now resides in Texas with her husband. You may contact her at SmitaTurakhia@gmail.com.

DATE LOANED	BORROWER'S NAME	DATE RETURNED